FIRST PRAYERS

Illustrated by

TASHA TUDOR

The Lutterworth Press

First published in Great Britain, 1964

This impression 1991
Reprinted 1994

(L)

The Lutterworth Press
P.O. Box 60
Cambridge CB1 2NT
England

ISBN 0 7188 0306 X

Printed in Hong Kong by Colorcraft Ltd

To
Virginia
Low
Paine

The Lord's Prayer

Our Father, Which art in
heaven,
Hallowed be Thy name.
Thy Kingdom come,
Thy will be done
in earth as it is in heaven.
Give us this day our daily bread,
and forgive us our trespasses
as we forgive them that
trespass against us,
And lead us not into temptation,
but deliver us from evil.
For Thine is the kingdom,
the power, and the glory,
for ever and ever. Amen.

A Morning Prayer

Through the night Thine angels kep
Watch around me while I slept.
Now the dark has gone away,
Lord, I thank Thee for the day.

In the Morning

Now I wake and see the light:
'Tis God has kept me through the night.
To Him I lift my voice and pray
That He will keep me through the day.

In the Morning

Father in Heaven, all through the night.
I have been sleeping, safe in Thy sight.
Father, I thank Thee; bless me I pray,
Bless me and keep me all through the
day.

Lord, teach me to love Thy children
everywhere, because
Thou art their father and mine.
Amen.

God bless all those that I love;
God bless all those that love me;
God bless all those that love those that
I love,
And all those that love those that
love me.

From an old New England sampler

For Those We Love

Bless, O Lord Jesus, my parents,
And all who love me and take care of me.
Make me loving to them,
Polite and obedient, helpful and kind.
Amen.

O Holy Jesus,
Most merciful Redeemer,
Friend and brother,
May I know Thee more clearly,
Love Thee more dearly,
And follow Thee more nearly.
Amen.

St. Richard of Chichester

God be in my head,
And in my understanding;
God be in mine eyes,
And in my looking;
God be in my mouth
And in my speaking;
God be in my heart,
And in my thinking;
God be at my end and at my departing

Sixteenth Century

God be in my head, and in my understanding
God be in mine eyes, and in my looking
God be in my mouth, and in my speaking
God be in my heart, and in my thinking

Dear God in Paradise
Look upon our sowing:
Bless the little gardens
And the green things growing.

Christ as a Light, illumine and guide
me,
Christ as a Shield o'ershadow and
cover me.
Christ be under me,
Christ be over me,
Christ be beside me on left hand and
on right.
Christ be before me, behind me,
about me,
Christ this day be within and without
me. Amen.

St. Patrick

Love
Faith
Kindness
Charity
Generosity
Helpfulness

Grace before and after Meals

Bless me, O Lord, and let my food
strengthen me to serve Thee,
for Jesus Christ's sake. Amen.

The New England Primer

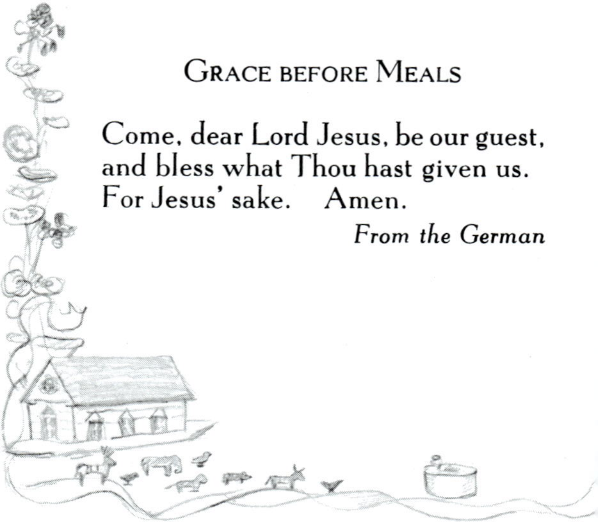

GRACE BEFORE MEALS

Come, dear Lord Jesus, be our guest,
and bless what Thou hast given us.
For Jesus' sake.   Amen.

From the German

Thou art great
And Thou art good,
And we thank Thee
For this food,
By Thy hand
Must all be fed,
And we thank Thee
For this bread.

T. Tudor

Grace before Meals

Bless us, O Lord, through these Thy gifts, and supply the wants of others.
Amen.

Gentle Jesus, Meek and Mild

Gentle Jesus, meek and mild,
Look upon a little child;
Pity my simplicity,
Suffer me to come to Thee.

Fain I would to Thee be brought;
Dearest God, forbid it not:
Give me, dearest God, a place
In the kingdom of Thy grace.

Put Thy hands upon my head,
Let me in Thine arms be stayed;
Let me lean upon Thy breast,
Lull me, lull me, Lord, to rest.

Hold me fast in Thy embrace,
Let me see Thy smiling face.
Give me, Lord, Thy blessing give
Pray for me, and I shall live.

Lamb of God, I look to Thee;
Thou shalt my Example be;
Thou art gentle, meek and mild,
Thou wast once a little Child.

Fain I would be as Thou art;
Give me Thy obedient heart.
Thou art pitiful and kind;
Let me have Thy loving mind.

Let me above all fulfil
God my heavenly Father's will;
Never His good Spirit grieve,
Only to His glory live.

Thou didst live to God alone,
Thou didst never seek Thine own;
Thou Thyself didst never please.
God was all Thy happiness.

Loving Jesu, gentle Lamb,
In Thy gracious hands I am,
Make me, Saviour, what Thou art,
Live Thyself within my heart.

Charles Wesley

Now the Day Is Over

Now the day is over,
Night is drawing nigh,
Shadows of the evening
Steal across the sky;

Jesus, give the weary
Calm and sweet repose;
With Thy tenderest blessing
May our eyelids close.

Grant to little children
Visions bright of Thee;
Guard the sailors tossing
On the deep blue sea.

Comfort every sufferer
Watching late in pain;
Those who plan some evil
From their sins restrain.

Through the long night watches,
May Thine angels spread
Their white wings above me,
Watching round my bed.

When the morning wakens,
Then may I arise
Pure and fresh and sinless
In Thy holy eyes.

Sabine Baring-Gould

JESUS, TENDER SHEPHERD

Jesus, tender Shepherd hear me;
Bless Thy little lamb tonight;
Through the darkness be Thou near
me,
Keep me safe till morning light.

All this day Thy hand has led me,
And I thank Thee for Thy care:
Thou has warmed me, clothed and
fed me;
Listen to my evening prayer!

Let my sins be all forgiven;
Bless the friends I love so well:
Take us all at last to heaven,
Happy there with Thee to dwell.

Mary Duncan

The Twenty-Third Psalm

The Lord is my shepherd; I shall not
want.
He maketh me to lie down in green
pastures:
He leadeth me beside the still waters.
He restoreth my soul: He leadeth me
in the paths of righteousness for His
name's sake.

Yea, though I walk through the valley of the shadow of death, I will fear no evil:
For Thou art with me; Thy rod and Thy staff they comfort me.
Thou preparest a table before me in the presence of mine enemies:
Thou anointest my head with oil;
My cup runneth over.
Surely goodness and mercy shall follow me all the days of my life:
And I will dwell in the house of the Lord for ever.

Matthew, Mark, Luke and John,
Bless the bed that I lie on.
Four corners to my bed,
Four angels round my head:
One to watch and one to pray,
And two to bear my soul away.

Cradle Hymn

Away in a manger, no crib for a bed,
The little Lord Jesus laid down His sweet head.
The stars in the bright sky looked down where He lay—
The little Lord Jesus asleep on the hay.

The cattle are lowing, the baby awakes,
But little Lord Jesus no crying He makes.
I love Thee, Lord Jesus! Look down
from the sky,
And stay by my cradle till morning is
nigh.

Be near me, Lord Jesus, I ask Thee to
stay
Close by me forever, and love me, I
pray.
Bless all the dear children, in Thy
tender care,
And take us to heaven, to live with
Thee there.

In the Evening

O, holy Father, I thank Thee for all the
blessings of this day. Forgive me that
which I have done wrong.
Bless me and keep me through the night,
for Jesus' sake.

Amen.

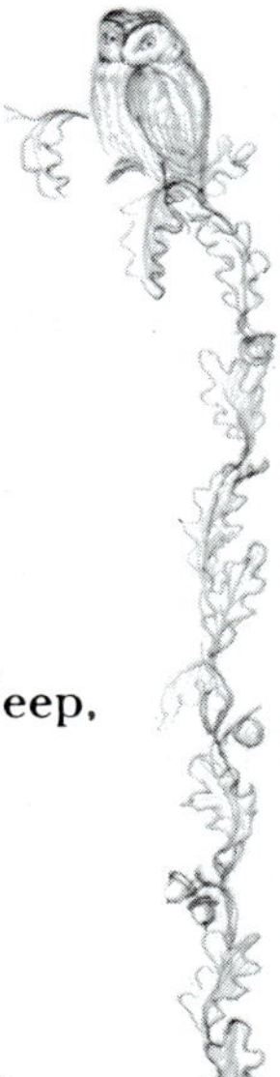

In the Evening

Lord, keep us safe this night,
Secure from all our fears.
May angels guard us while we sleep,
Till morning light appears.

The Lord bless us, and keep us.
The Lord make His face to shine upon
us, and be gracious unto us.
The Lord lift up His countenance upon us,
and give us peace, both now and
evermore.

Amen.